HOW DOES IT WORK?

LIGHT BULBS

by Mari Schuh

I0801925

pogo

Ideas for Parents and Teachers

Pogo Books let children practice reading informational text while introducing them to nonfiction features such as headings, labels, sidebars, maps, and diagrams, as well as a table of contents, glossary, and index.

Carefully leveled text with a strong photo match offers early fluent readers the support they need to succeed.

Before Reading

- "Walk" through the book and point out the various nonfiction features. Ask the student what purpose each feature serves.
- Look at the glossary together. Read and discuss the words.

Read the Book

- Have the child read the book independently.
- Invite him or her to list questions that arise from reading.

After Reading

- Discuss the child's questions. Talk about how he or she might find answers to those questions.
- Prompt the child to think more. Ask: Do you know what kinds of light bulbs are used in your home? Where are they used?

Pogo Books are published by Jump!
5357 Penn Avenue South
Minneapolis, MN 55419
www.jumplibrary.com

Copyright © 2021 Jump!
International copyright reserved in all countries.
No part of this book may be reproduced in any form without written permission from the publisher.

Library of Congress Cataloging-in-Publication Data

Names: Schuh, Mari C., 1975- author.
Title: Light bulbs / by Mari Schuh.
Description: Minneapolis, MN: Jump!, Inc., [2021]
Series: How does it work?
Includes index. | Audience: Ages 7-10
Identifiers: LCCN 2020028524 (print)
LCCN 2020028525 (ebook)
ISBN 9781645277774 (hardcover)
ISBN 9781645277781 (paperback)
ISBN 9781645277798 (ebook)
Subjects: LCSH: Light bulbs—Juvenile literature.
Classification: LCC TK4351 .S38 2021 (print)
LCC TK4351 (ebook) | DDC 621.32—dc23
LC record available at https://lccn.loc.gov/2020028524
LC ebook record available at https://lccn.loc.gov/2020028525

Editor: Eliza Leahy
Designer: Molly Ballanger

Photo Credits: Yastrebinsky/Dreamstime, cover; AvailableLight/iStock, 1; gresei/Shutterstock, 3; michellegibson/Getty, 4; SolStock/iStock, 5; Science & Society Picture Library/Getty, 6-7; EHStockphoto/Shutterstock, 8 (left); Bamidor/Shutterstock, 8 (right); Altaoosthuizen/Dreamstime, 9; monkeybusinessimages/iStock, 10-11; Parilov/Shutterstock, 12-13; Roman Rybaleov/Shutterstock, 14; JGI/Jamie Grill/Getty, 15; Simon Kadula/Shutterstock, 16; Welcomia/Dreamstime, 16-17; Chat Karen Studio/Shutterstock, 18-19; Andrey_Popov/Shutterstock, 20-21; Arti_Zav/Shutterstock, 23.

Printed in the United States of America at Corporate Graphics in North Mankato, Minnesota.

TABLE OF CONTENTS

CHAPTER 1

LIGHT UP THE DARK

You wake up thirsty. It is dark. You flip the light switch. Now you can safely walk to the kitchen.

We use light bulbs every day to help us see. They are in lamps, flashlights, and cars. They are in **appliances** such as microwaves and ovens. They also light up streets and parks.

In 1879, Joseph Swan made an **incandescent** light bulb. But it burned out too quickly.

Later in 1879, Thomas Edison also made a light bulb. He used a different material. The bulb burned longer. This bulb is similar to those we use today.

DID YOU KNOW?

Before the light bulb, people used candles and **kerosene** lamps. These provided a flame for light. But the flames were not very bright. Candles and lamps could tip over and start fires.

Joseph Swan's light
Thomas Edison's light

CHAPTER 2

HOW THEY WORK

How does an incandescent light bulb work? It changes **electricity** into light energy. Electricity comes into buildings through wires. It powers lights, computers, and much more.

To make light, electricity flows to a bulb. Then it flows to a thin, coiled wire inside. The wire is called a **filament**.

The filament gets very hot. It gives off heat. It gets so hot that it glows. This creates light.

DID YOU KNOW?

Light bulbs are ranked by the amount of energy they use. They are also ranked by the amount of light they give off. The energy is measured in **watts**. The light is measured in **lumens**.

The glass bulb keeps **oxygen** away from the filament. Why is this important? If oxygen touches the filament, the filament will burn out.

The air inside the bulb is **inert gas**. It keeps the filament from getting too hot. It keeps it from burning out.

TAKE A LOOK!

What are the parts of a light bulb? Take a look!

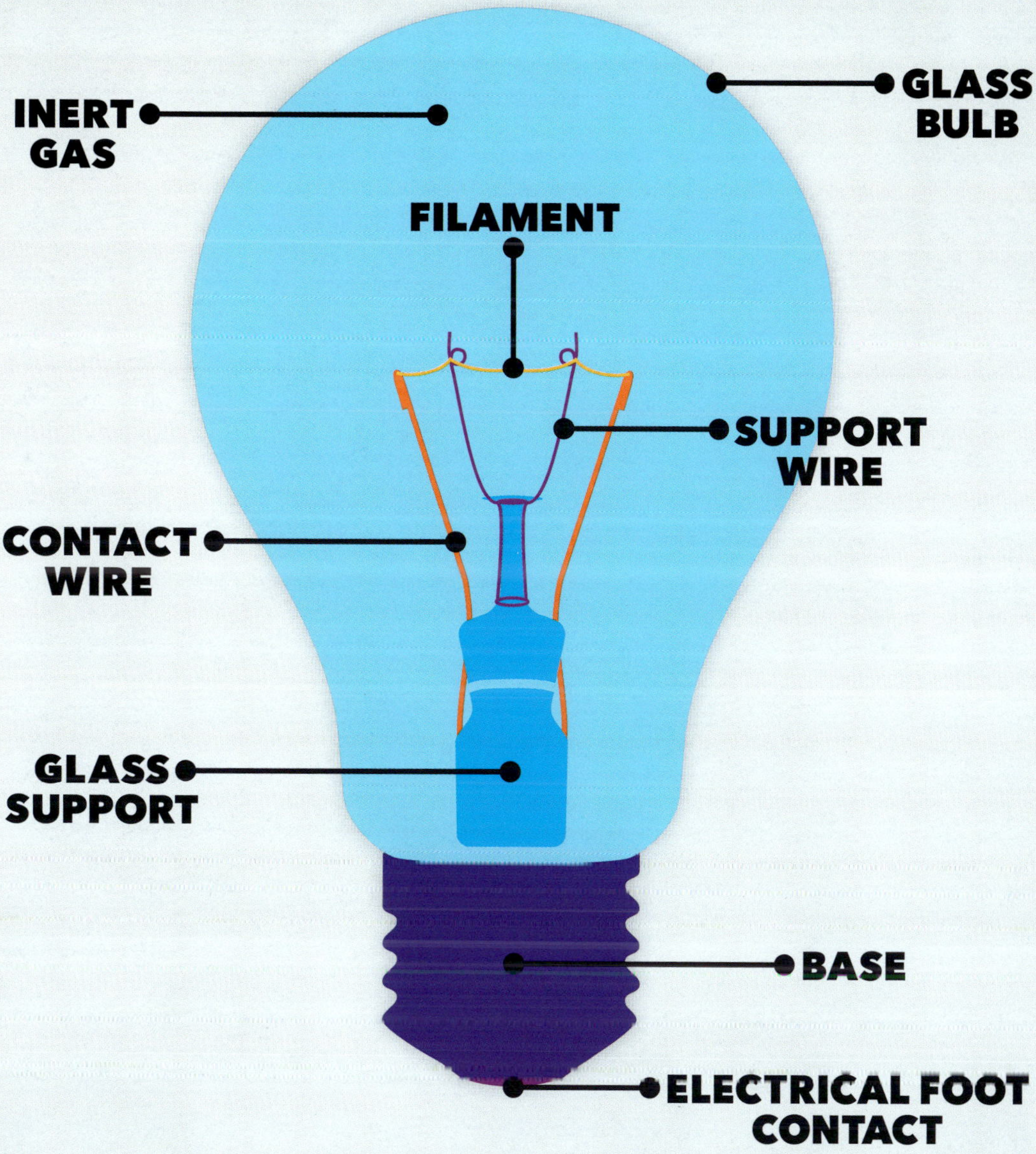

CHAPTER 3

ALL KINDS OF BULBS

Incandescent bulbs last about one year. They waste a lot of energy heating the filament to make it glow.

Some light bulbs are **efficient**. The materials in them help them use less energy. The bulbs often cost more. But they last longer. Compact fluorescent lamps (CFLs) are efficient bulbs. They don't waste as much heat energy. They can last up to 10 years!

Halogen bulbs are another kind. They are very bright. Because of this, they are often used outdoors. Car headlights usually use these bulbs.

Light-emitting diodes (LEDs) are a third option. They cost more than other bulbs. But they can last 15 years or more! Most LEDs shine light on a specific area.

TAKE A LOOK!

Some light bulbs are more efficient than others. Take a look!

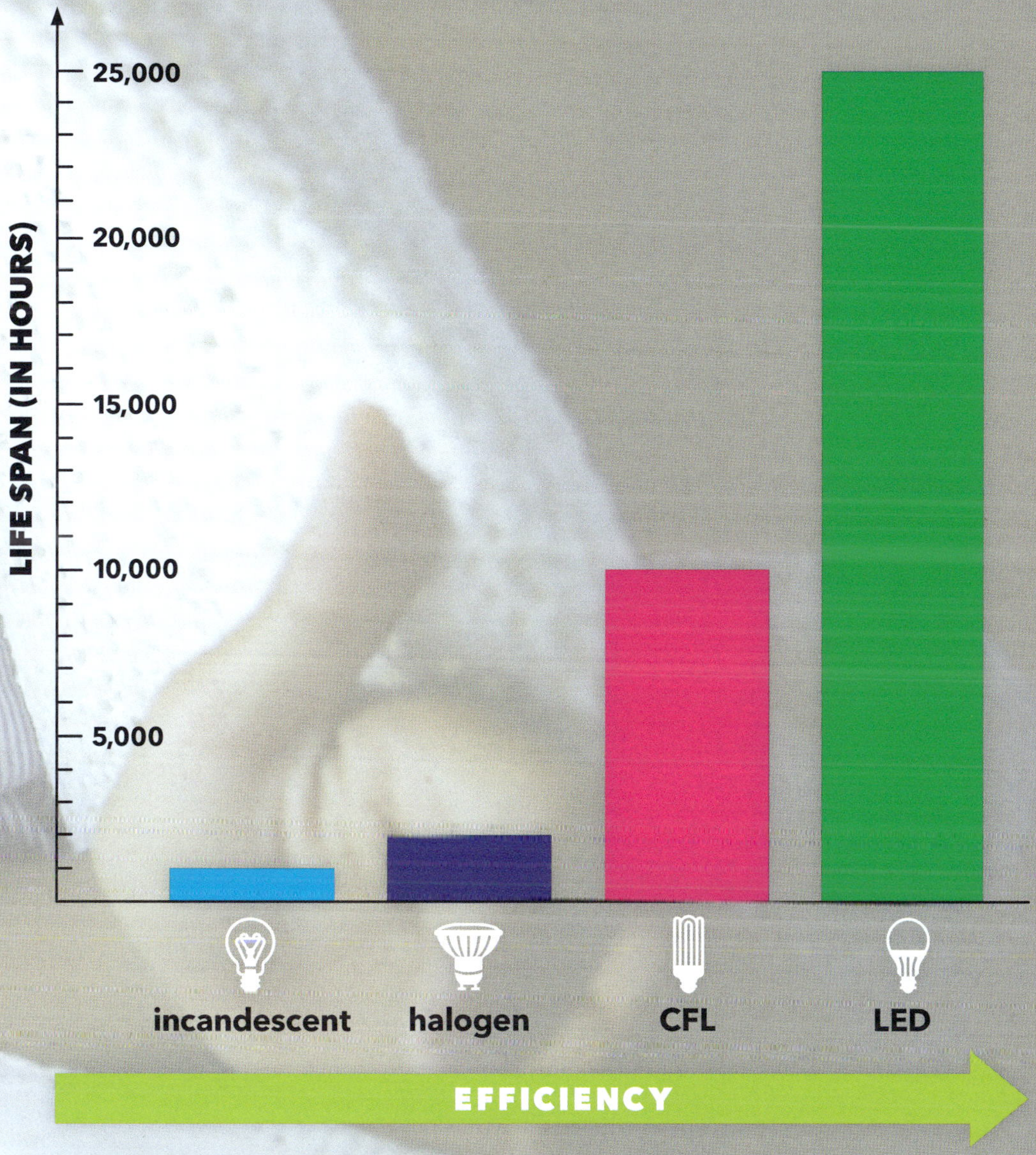

SETTINGS
SCHEDULE
Color
Intensity

Some light bulbs can be controlled from anywhere! How? You can use a smartphone or other device. You can put lights on a schedule. You can even control some with your voice! Others turn on when they sense **motion**.

Companies work to make better bulbs. How might light bulbs change in the future?

ACTIVITIES & TOOLS

TRY THIS!

COMPARE LIGHT BULBS

In this activity, compare the light and heat that incandescent and CFL bulbs give off. Both bulbs need to have the same number of lumens. To find out the numbers, check the light bulbs or the boxes they came in.

What You Need:

- one incandescent bulb
- lamp
- thermometer
- ruler
- timer or stopwatch
- pen or pencil
- one CFL bulb

1. **Have an adult put the incandescent light bulb in the lamp. Turn on the lamp. Notice how much light it gives off.**
2. **Hold a thermometer about six inches (15 cm) above the light bulb for one minute. Write down the temperature.**
3. **Turn off the lamp. Wait for the light bulb to cool. Ask the adult to remove the light bulb.**
4. **Have the adult put the CFL bulb in the lamp. Turn on the lamp. Notice how much light it gives off.**
5. **Hold a thermometer about six inches (15 cm) above the light bulb for one minute. Write down the temperature. Did one bulb make more light than the other? Did one make more heat than the other?**

GLOSSARY

appliances: Machines created to do certain jobs; toasters, washing machines, and hair dryers are appliances.

efficient: Using less energy to perform a task.

electricity: A form of energy that can be used to make light, heat, and motion.

filament: A very thin wire in an incandescent light bulb that heats and glows when electricity goes through it.

incandescent: Glowing with a bright light and heat.

inert gas: Gas that does not go through chemical reactions.

kerosene: A type of oil that is burned as fuel.

lumens: Units for measuring brightness.

motion: An act of changing place or position.

oxygen: A colorless gas in the air that people and animals breathe.

watts: Units for measuring electrical power.

INDEX

TO LEARN MORE

Finding more information is as easy as 1, 2, 3.

1. Go to www.factsurfer.com
2. Enter "lightbulbs" into the search box.
3. Choose your book to see a list of websites.

FACT SURFER